Wide Open

Wide Open

On Living with Passion and Purpose

Dawna Markova, Ph.D.

Conari Press

First published in 2008 by Conari Press,
an imprint of Red Wheel/Weiser, LLC
With offices at:
500 Third Street, Suite 230
San Francisco, CA 94107
www.redwheelweiser.com

ISBN: 978-1-57324-407-7
Library of Congress Cataloging-in-Publication Data is available upon request.

Cover and text design by Donna Linden
Typeset in Artcraft and Perpetua
Cover photograph © Corbis
Text photographs: Pages 2, 6, 10, 38, 52, 65, 71, 73, 76, 113 © Corbis; Pages 9, 63, 68, 126 © iStockphoto.com; Page 14 © John Woodworth/iStockphoto.com; Pages 16, 26, 41, 47, 57, 60, 97 © Anthony Ise/PhotoDisc; Pages 21, 37, 84, 100 © Alison Miksch/Brand Pictures; Page 24 © Tanya Shkondina/iStockphoto.com; Page 29 © Christopher Steer/iStockphoto.com; Page 32 © Brandon Alms/iStockphoto.com; Page 35 © Kostyantyn Kurhan/iStockphoto.com; Page 44 © Chanyut Sribuarawd/iStockphoto.com; Page 49 © Elena Elisseeva/iStockphoto.com; Page 58 © Anna Yu/iStockphoto.com; Page 74 © Pedro Tavares/iStockphoto.com; Page 79 © Robert Kohlhuber/iStockphoto.com; Page 81 © Maxim Petrichuk/iStockphoto.com; Page 89 © Emilia Stasiak/iStockphoto.com; Page 92 © Andrejs Zemdega/iStockphoto.com; Page 105 © Sergei Sverdelov/iStockphoto.com; Page 108 © Hans F. Meier/iStockphoto.com; Page 116 © Susan Fox/iStockphoto.com; Page 121 © Larissa Skinner/iStockphoto.com; Page 122 © Sherri Camp/iStockphoto.com

Printed in Hong Kong
SS
10 9 8 7 6 5 4 3 2 1

MAY WE INSPIRE OURSELVES
AND EACH OTHER TO SERVE LIFE.

Contents

Opening Wider

When I wrote *I Will Not Die an Unlived Life* in 1999, it was as my personal journal, a "paper mirror" to the conversations I was having with myself on a six-month winter retreat at a tiny cabin in the snow-buried mountains of Utah. I was there because my life had flattened into a list and my body and soul needed to catch up with my mind. I had no idea how to be in my own company without the external stimulation of media or someone else's needs to attend to. The only companions I took with me were a golden retriever and a vapor trail of questions that could not be answered.

In the years since the book was published, people all over the world have written to me to tell me that it inspired in them a passion to live wide open. They told me its unanswerable questions helped them have inspiring conversations with themselves. They reported that the stories encouraged them to live on purpose instead of just letting life happen to them. The book has been translated into many languages. I still have trouble believing that something so personal could help people I have never met find their own truth.

I think of the poem that seeded that book as a candle. It sheds light on the ways to live a life with passion, on purpose. I do not know if it, like a child, came through me for others, or just for me. I do not know why people in Singapore and Syracuse have read it, posted it on their refrigerators and walls, tucked it into boxes of seeds, passed it from one open hand to another.

Since the publication of the book, I have wanted to place a kiss into the palm of each person who has written to me as well as those who have carried the book and the poem around like a secret friend. The little volume you are holding is the closest I can come. It celebrates the ripple of recognition we have created together.

When I was alone in the cabin, writing *I Will Not Die an Unlived Life,* one of the ways I befriended myself was by cutting squares of fabric from favorite clothes I no longer wore, arranging them into a new pattern and sewing a quilt to comfort me in the long, dark Utah nights. I followed a similar process in crafting this book: I snipped quotes, concepts, and bits of wisdom from the original book and paired them with evocative questions that had inspired and opened my mind. I wove them all together with blessings for the future that arose when I thought of you, the reader, holding this book.

There are many people in this particular time of history who, like me, are feeling disconnected from a world that pours forth anguish like rain. I know there are others who need to learn to live in an interdependent, diverse, ever-changing world, where breakdown of everything we have counted on is daily fare.

Another thing I know is that we all need inspiration now. In times of great change, people reach for meaning because meaning brings strength. When we don't have a sense of purpose, when we don't know what we love, what gifts we bring, and what we truly serve, we create lives and workplaces that are fundamentally meaningless and devoid of vitality. We stop listening to the deepest aspects of ourselves and each other. We stop learning how to fill ourselves from the ordinary events of our lives. We become solitary bystanders rather than full participants in life.

This little book is meant to help you be in conversation with what is hidden in you in such a way that you awaken to your life as the blessing it truly is. It is meant to support you in the exploration of what can bring you more alive and fruitful, and in the consideration of what really matters and how you really matter to the rest of us.

After four decades of midwifing people's gifts, talents, and dreams, what has become obvious to me is that the quest for purpose and passion brings more value to us than the destination we finally reach. After we grow up, life asks us to grow forward. Inevitably, this questing draws you deeper into yourself as well as into the world.

Creating lives that are empowering rather than imprisoning means asking yourself some very challenging questions: How can I bring forth the gifts and talents that are hidden in me and others? What do I truly love and value about life? What are the environments and rhythms that bring out the best in me?

These are some of the questions that open the mind's gateway to reveal the wisdom that is right below the surface of our everyday lives. I offer this book as a companion to your journey. Let one of the questions become a polestar that you ask yourself first thing in the morning. Rather than trying to answer it, sit with it, shower with it, have breakfast with it; let your mind wander with it as you walk and work. Check in on the question from time to time and then let it wander off as you wonder what it has to teach you.

"How do I live divided no more?" was my focal point in this way for two weeks. After a short time of noticing where my mind drifted to when I asked it, I began to draw whatever image came to me or journal the sensations I felt in my body and the stories that arose in my mind. Sometimes,

I used the question as a rhythm setter for snowshoeing, one word for each breath. I wrote it down in a notebook before I went to sleep, giving it over to my dreaming mind.

You can use one of the questions within these pages as a starting place for a conversation you have with someone you love or someone you work with or someone you barely know. When that question is no longer interesting to you, begin with a new inquiry. Each of these evocative questions is meant to help open the uncharted territories of your inner world. They hold the possibility of orienting you toward what your life is asking of you and what you are asking of life.

I invite you to pick out a specific question or just flip through the pages and let one call out to you. Then wander and wonder with it. Go for a walk, take a shower, hit some golf balls, cook a meal, drive on a back country road, doodle on a pad, write in your journal. Every once in a while, bring your mind back to the question, curious as a young child. Listen with wonder to the stories that emerge in response to these questions, stories about who you are, the challenges you've faced to build what you've built, the feelings, fears, learnings and discoveries you have gathered through your life.

Purpose is the activating intelligence that guides our life. It is distilled from the stories and ideas that emerge from these big wide conversations we have with ourselves. It emerges from the yearning in each of us to create meaning and wholeness.

May the conversations that are born from this book inspire you, dear reader, to open your heart and mind to all that you can make possible in this world.

Dawna Markova
Northern California, 2008

Wide Open

I will not die an unlived life.
I will not live in fear
of falling or catching fire.
I choose to inhabit my days,
to allow my living to open me,
to make me less afraid,
more accessible,
to loosen my heart
until it becomes a wing,
a torch, a promise.
I choose to risk my significance;
to live so that which came to me as seed
goes to the next as blossom
and that which came to me as blossom,
goes on as fruit.

Living with Purpose and Passion

After realizing how much of his energy he had used to stay out of life instead of participating in it, Nobel prize-winning poet Octavio Paz wrote a remarkable poem entitled "After." The story I tell myself is that it was a response to questions his soul was asking of him: "How do I live in the great gift of life without hesitation, ambivalence, or reservation? How do I live without pushing life or love away?" Because the poem so impassioned him with its truth, he read it to himself every morning and evening for the rest of his life as an inspiration to live wide open.

The night after my father died with a shrug, similar questions rose to the surface of my mind on a surging tide of grief. How could I cross the abyss of despair that swallowed my father? How could I live so that my life would have meaning and so that I could bring meaning to life?

My tears turned to ink. The words that flowed out of my pen were a response to these questions. Perhaps they were a blessing from my father. Certainly they became a bridge across that abyss. The poem has become a light I've followed for a quarter of a century. It has led me through cancer, chaos, and despondency. It reminds me still who I am, what I serve, and why I am here.

Inspired by Octavio Paz, I say the poem to inspire myself each morning before my feet hit the floor. Each evening I whisper it to make meaning of the moments I have lived.

What is the unlived life that is calling to you?

It's never too late to become what you might have been.
—**George Eliot**

May you open fully to all that life is offering to you.

Thinking Yourself Home

No one can tell you how to find your purpose. It can only emerge slowly, in your own dark sky, in whatever territory is sacred to you, be that church or woods. It can't be found by searching for a role model. It is seldom discovered by following anyone else's rules. It lives in the rest in the place where music is born—the fertile void, the silence between notes. It emerges slowly as a sunrise as we search through our gifts, our darkness, our losses and loves. Your job and mine is to be quiet and alone from time. To be present to ourselves and the natural world, and to be in conversation with what is hidden in us to explore what brings us more alive.

What is it too soon for?

What is it too late for?

What is it just the right time for?

Meaning is not something you stumble across, like the answer to a riddle or the prize in a treasure hunt. Meaning is something you build into your life. You build it out of your own past, out of your affections and loyalties, out of the experience of humankind as it is passed on to you, out of your own talent and people you love, out of the values for which you are willing to sacrifice. You are the only one who can put it together into that unique pattern that will be your life. Let it be a life that has dignity and meaning for you. If it does, then the particular balance of success or failure is of no account.

—*John Gardner*

May you allow yourself stillness so you can
open your mind to your deepest truth.

Losing Yourself to Find Yourself

You don't have to be in a life-threatening situation to ignite your passion to live. Some of us are called to it by numbness, fatigue, or boredom. Some of us have the sense that we're not using ourselves to the utmost. Even at our happiest moments, we may feel that something is missing.

To explore what it would mean to live fully, sensually alive and passionately on purpose, you have to drop your preconceived ideas of who and what you are. In the fists of our minds, we clutch stories, explanations, and interpretations of our identities so tightly that we become numb. What are we holding onto, anyway? How much do you want your mind to be free? How much do you want your heart and soul to be free—free of and free from struggle, free from doubt in the canyons of your bones? How much do you want to be free in the home of your own heart and mind?

Who are you when you are not being productive?

Who were you before the alarm clock rang this morning?

Who are you in your dreams?

Who is the "you" that notices your thoughts?

The seed that is to grow
must lose itself as seed;
And they that creep
may graduate through
chrysalis to wings.

Wilt thou then, O mortal,
cling to husks which
falsely seem to you
the self?
—Wu Ming Fu, twelfth century

May you create the inner spaciousness you need to allow a moment of rest when all thoughts fly above you like kites in a strong wind.

A Second Innocence

Retreating into yourself to find purpose can be like straddling a dock and a boat that is moving away. We are pulled in opposite directions by the intense desire of the mind for human involvement and the equally intense need of the soul for its own company. In the sheer immensity of solitude, when one can no longer draw energy from external sources, we come to see how much of what we habitually call being productive is merely the evasion of sitting still and meeting what is most difficult for us to receive with compassion—our own pain.

So many of us are afraid of meeting ourselves without distraction. We have been taught to fashion an image of who we think we are supposed to be. This fear of knowing who we really are causes us to sidestep our own destiny, leaving us hungry in a famine of our own making. Each of us is here to give something that only we can offer. When we avoid knowing ourselves, we end up living numb, passionless lives, disconnected from our soul's true purpose.

How can you even know your truth unless you slow down, in your own quiet company? When the inner walls to our souls are graffitied with advertisements, commercials, and the opinions of everyone who has ever known and labeled us, turning inward requires a major clean-up.

Where does your mind go when you sit in
a still moment under an immense sky?

For it is only framed in space that beauty blooms. A candle flowers in the space of night. . . .My life lacks this quality of significance, and therefore beauty, because there is so little empty space. There are so few empty pages in my engagement pad or empty hours in which to stand alone and find myself.

—Anne Morrow Lindbergh

May you give yourself your own undivided attention.

Divided No More

It's not pain that is so hard on our souls, but rather the meaningless suffering that comes from feeling disconnected from a sense of purpose. Purpose is like a constellation: it can only be glimpsed in darkness, but it is always there as a homing device. Just as geese have an internal capacity to follow coastlines and the magnetic resonance of the Earth to tell them where to go, we need to follow the yearnings of our heart and soul to find our way. We need to stay faithful to the quest for what is original and authentic in ourselves. Ultimately we have nothing else with which to make or unmake the whole world.

We all feel a tremendous push from the past and a compelling pull from the future to step fully into who we are meant to be. We need courage and time to reorder our priorities and consider this internal exploration as important as "work" and outward success. We need to practice the art of stripping away false notions about who we think we are so that we can deal with what is real. We need to release anything that is deadening to our spirits. We need to stand for something that is greater than ourselves.

In your own history, what has been the best rhythm
and way for you to come to know your own truth?

*The antidote to exhaustion may not be rest. It may
be wholeheartedness. You are so exhausted because all
of the things you are doing are just busyness. There's
a central core of wholeheartedness totally missing from
what you're doing.*

—Brother David Steindl-Rast

May you create the inner spaciousness you need
in order to hear all that life is asking of you.

Living On Purpose

The crises of our lives remind us that we need to inhale, to create the kind of spaciousness that enables us to live from the inside out again, to find joy again, as well as tenderness toward ourselves and the world.

Perhaps *find* is the wrong word. I don't think anyone "finds" joy or tenderness. Rather, we cultivate them by searching for the preciousness of small things, the ordinary miracles that strengthen our hearts, enabling us to stay open to what is difficult. It can be as simple as our delight in taking a shower or a slow walk that has no destination, in touching something soft, in noticing the one small black bird who sings every morning from the top of a big old pine tree. We need to give our attention to the simple things that give us pleasure with the same fervor we give to the complex things that drive us crazy.

What surprises you in your current life?

What inspires and moves you?

Self care is never a selfish act—it is simply good steward-ship of the only gift I was put on earth to offer to others. Any time we can listen to our true self, and give it the care it requires, we do so not only for ourselves, but for the many others whose lives we touch.

—Parker Palmer

May you find your true wealth in the
simple moments you are living now.

Mental Metabolism

We all have islands of fear inside us, but we also all have continents of wisdom and truth. How do we find our way to them when all we know of the inner world is lists of things to do or criticisms of things we have done? Without knowing how to journey beyond these, our lives remain unlived, unexplored.

Certain kinds of questions evoke the purpose and passion that are always alive in the deep darkness of our intuitive minds. They can cause us to step back from seeing the tiny details and dots of our daily existence, and help us perceive the whole picture, the deeper meaning of who we are and why we are alive. They take us on the journey from emptiness to openness, from wonder to wisdom. Have you ever had a question that was really puzzling you and stepped into a shower, forgetting the question, but as you stepped out and toweled off, it popped into your mind in a whole new way? I call that "mental metabolism," which refers to the mind's ability to intuitively digest our question without our being consciously aware of it.

Who stands behind you and prayed that you would be born?

Who dreamt that someday there would be one such as you?

Who stands beside you supporting you?

Who will come after you, thanking you

for what you've done and who you have been?

We are now at a point in time when the ability to receive, utilize, store, transform and transmit data—the lowest cognitive form—has expanded literally beyond comprehension. Understanding and wisdom are largely forgotten as we struggle under an avalanche of data and information.

—Dee Hock, Birth of the Chaordic Age

May you be caught and held by hidden hands.

Questing Inward

Questions can be dangerous. They can take us right to the edge of what is known and comfortable. They can require tremendous courage to ask, because we know that new questions can lead to new ways of perceiving, and new perceptions can lead to new explorations and actions. Pick any "dangerous" question you have been avoiding asking yourself and you'll see what I mean. A question such as, "How do I make my work too small for me?" or "Is my spirit dying in my relationship?" or poet Mary Oliver's magnificently disturbing, "What is it that you want to do with the one, wild, precious thing called your life?" The asking of such questions often leads to the perilous, growing edge of our minds.

All new thought begins with a dangerous question that pries our hearts and minds open and rescues us from the numbness of fear and cynicism. It can return us to a second innocence where we can listen to the truth about what we really feel and wake up.

What is the first question that you ask yourself every morning?

I don't know who or what put the question, I don't know when it was put. I don't even remember answering. But at some moment I did answer Yes to Someone— or Something—and from that hour I was certain that existence is meaningful and that, therefore, my life, in self-surrender, had a goal.

—Dag Hammarskjöld

May you find the courage you need to ask yourself the questions that will free your mind and strengthen your soul.

Embracing the Mystery

Can we embrace the unanswered? Can we live in the mystery? What is required is remembering what we knew as young children in our most fertile learning state. Spend ten minutes with a three-year-old and you'll see what I mean, or read the diaries of some of the greatest minds in history—Albert Einstein, Virginia Woolf, Aldous Huxley, Howard Thurman—and you'll discover them asking wide and open questions of themselves, pondering and playing in them for years.

Traveling from the known to the unknown requires crossing an abyss of emptiness. We first experience disorientation and confusion. Then, if we are willing to cross in wonder, we enter an expansive and untamed country that has its own rhythm. Time melts. Thoughts become stories, music, poems, images, ideas. This is the intelligence of the heart—a vast range of receptive and connective abilities: intuition, wisdom, meaning making. It is aesthetic, qualitative, creative, sensitive, innovative. And it is here that we uncover our purpose and passion. The future exists only in our imaginations.

It is a collective story waiting to be expressed. That can only happen if we are willing to enter that emptiness and listen in the silence for a future we can befriend.

If you knew you couldn't fail, how would you live?

This is the charged, the dangerous moment, when every-thing must be re-examined, must be made new, when nothing at all can be taken for granted.

—James Baldwin

May your quest for purpose be compassionate
and like a pebble ripple into the middle of this moment.

Landscapes of the Mind

Whether we know it or not, we all are storytellers. We take a bit of experience and stretch or shrink it into a story that makes meaning and determines what actions we will take or inhibit. My back is twingeing as I sit here. Sensation. The data of my current experience. Then comes a story. "I must have pulled a muscle skiing." Or "I probably have a tumor on my spine." Or, "It's my husband Andy's fault for not letting me sleep on the side of the bed I wanted to last night." If I'm not aware that I am creating these stories, they direct my actions. But once I give attention to the space between impulse and action, I can notice these stories that shape my experience and choose my response.

As with any other great force of nature, there is both glory and danger in the stories we tell ourselves. Some are toxic and keep our problems festering. Others are tonic and carry us beyond the limitations of our previous history. To be in a life of our own definition, we must be able to discover which stories we are following and chose the ones that help us grow the most interesting possibilities.

This sounds so simple as I just rattle it off, and it is simple, but oh, it is not easy. These compelling stories make us deaf to anything except the rumblings of our sacred hungers—the need to be loved, to have someone be with us, to be acknowledged as making a difference.

What story are you telling yourself about
the challenges in your life right now?

....

*We make our lives bigger or smaller, more expansive or
more limited, according to the interpretation of life that
is our story.*

—Christina Baldwin

....

May the sacred hungers of your body and soul be nourished.

Rut to River

When one stage of our lives is complete, we are at an intersection, a threshold. Because we are all such creative beings in essence, we approach the unknown, stories first. Like Rumpelstiltskin, we take any bit of straw, any fact of reality—for example, "My son is going away to school"—and then either spin it into gold or dung by the stories we choose to attach to it: "He won't need me. Nobody needs me. I'm gonna go eat worms," or "He and I will each learn whole new ways of relating to the world." I call the former "rut stories" because they numb us and confirm that we always are who we always have been; I call the latter "river stories," because I think of them as energizing, carrying us toward purpose and possibility.

Usually we don't even realize we are telling ourselves these stories, but they shape our entire way of perceiving, believing, and relating. Just track your mind for a few minutes and uncover yours for yourself.

What are the rut stories, the limiting beliefs that you
habitually tell yourself? What would the river story
be that would shift the axis of your existence so that
you could live more alive, serving your purpose?

---

*The stories people tell have a way of taking care of them.
If stories come to you, care for them and learn to give them
away where they are needed. Sometimes a person needs a
story more than food to stay alive. That is why we put these
stories in each other's memories.*

—Barry Lopez

May you let go of the too-small circles
you have drawn around yourself and others.

Passion's Sleep

In my better moments, I think of emptiness as passion's sleep. In my worse moments, when I'm trying to avoid or get rid of that emptiness, I call it inertia, feeling lazy, depressed, or useless. Ultimately, it always seems to request the same thing—that I withdraw into solitude as much as possible, that I integrate what was, and get receptive to what is: my present experience, rhythm, body, the natural world, to what could be needed by the larger community, to what is being asked of me by a possible future.

Physicist Niels Bohr said that the opposite of a profound truth is not a lie, but rather another profound truth. That's why, in order to know passion, we must also know its opposite truth. Only this way can we craft lives that are wider, fiercer, and more tender, where there is more space for discovery of what can be possible. Thinking this way, what does inertia become? Drop the label. Welcome the energy as it is instead of pushing it away. Soften your awareness and open to it instead of trying to ignore it.

You may discover that inertia is a form of a larger intelligence. If we only experienced passion, we would be bold beyond belief, but we would burn, burn, burn ourselves out in a rapturous relationship with the untamable within us. We also need the dark, the stillness, the quiet of the night for the stars and constellations to appear, the patterns of movement of the whole universe to be visible.

How can you best move yourself through inertia to passion?

My strength is gone. When I lie down worn out, others will stand, young and fresh. By the stairs I have built, they will mount. They will never know the name of the person who made them. At the clumsy work they will laugh; when the stones roll, they will curse me. But they will mount, and on my work, they will climb and by my stair.

—Olive Shreiner

May you learn to breathe your spirit alive.

Sacred Hungers

Listen into the silence of inertia. What you may hear is a hunger, a keening in the emptiness. Not a hunger of the body, but rather the sound of a sacred hunger, the desire to germinate that is within every seed in the soul. It is the calling of talents and potentialities that wait to bud in the dark recesses of ourselves, beneath the static and cacophony of everyday life. It is the calling for some essential needs to be filled: to express and receive love; to be present with and for what we love; to know and be known; to be peaceful and satisfied; to be acknowledged as making a difference and acknowledge that others make a difference to us; to find meaning and purpose in life as well as having life find meaning in our existence.

If you move very fast and stay very busy living in a very noisy way, you may never even hear these hungers. But if you let yourself be still, if you are willing to explore the dark shadows on the other side of passion, you will hear them. Because the seeds of life that are in all of us want to expand outward. The shell around each seed that grows thick to protect it must crack if that seed is to sprout. What is known and familiar must fall away. And just as you can hear your stomach grumbling when your body is hungry, so, if you listen deeply in the silence, you will hear your soul keening. Sacred hungers keep pushing at our edges, wanting us to let go of the old ways we have kept ourselves secure so we can expand into blossoming the life force of what we love.

What is the name you call yourself
when you want your soul to answer?

Let yourself be silently drawn by the stronger pull
of what you really love.

—Rumi

May your life be a mirror for the beauty you find in the world.

The Open Heart

Befriending oneself sometimes involves opening your heart as a homeless shelter for all the exiled aspects of your being that you have been running from for years without even knowing that's what you have been doing. Befriending yourself involves telling yourself the complete truth about everything and challenging the thinking that says horrible things will happen as a result. Is it really true that you will be rejected if you don't respond to all the emails or phone calls you receive? Ultimately, befriending yourself means finding the courage to become a refuge for whatever is most difficult for you to accept. Not courage as in blood and guts, but rather courage to root in one's darkness and allow a sense of understanding to grow there.

Reconnecting with who you really are in this way is a stepping stone for understanding the experience of other people. It is how we grow compassion. Your pain begins to have meaning. When you allow your heart and mind to pay attention to each other in this way, silence becomes a loom on which your soul can weave the fabric of purpose into your life.

What are the courageous conversations
you need to have with yourself?

What are the conditions you need to create to have them?

•

*If you bring forth what is within you, what you bring forth
will save you. If you do not bring forth what is within you,
what you do not bring forth will destroy you.*

—Jesus, Gospel of Saint Thomas

May you open your heart to yourself in wonder and mercy.

Passion's Seasons

Anything capable of decay is also capable of regeneration. Passion is a given when we are young. As children we burn with it, until it gets smothered or beaten out of us. But as adults, passion can become so elusive. We hear it as if there were thin ribbony veils of music playing someplace just beyond what we can perceive, pale and near-transparent. How do we evoke the untamable in ourselves? How do we open fully to that passion, letting it lift us and carry us forward?

Passion breaks us open until there is no partition between our body and the body of the world. It acts on us until something takes root inside and insists on growing. It begins as a reaching down into the dark of inertia as well as up and out toward the light. Passion is the capacity to touch and be touched, to reach out and to let in. It may require that you break your heart open so wide that it can contain the whole world. If you break the word *passion* apart, it becomes three words: Pass I On. It creates the desire to reach, to pass on to the world what you love. And through that opening, the world passes into you.

How can you evoke the untamable in yourself,
the part that dreams and imagines beyond what is known?

No punishment anyone might inflict on us could possibly be worse than the punishment we inflict on ourselves by conspiring in our own diminishment.

—Parker Palmer

May you parent your passion exquisitely.

Rekindling the Flame

Rekindling the flame of our passion requires melting the frozen ice floes that block us from nurturing what we truly love. Rather than trying to be secure by merely keeping ourselves alive, the relevant focus of our passion needs to become taking the necessary risks so that the thing in us that loves, and the things it loves, stay alive and are passed on.

Were you taught that you shouldn't enjoy anything too much because you'll hurt too much when you lose it? The reality is that whether or not we enjoy it, we do lose everything eventually. We lose it all. All the more reason, therefore, to enjoy our passion, to love what we love, to store up the sweetness, so we become strong enough to stay present with the pain of loss when it inevitably comes.

Perhaps we fear passion because it is, in essence, out of our control, beyond our reasonable and known selves. At the same time, we yearn for the flame, the dimension, the pulse. Always, passion reveals the back side of our hearts, our blessed wildness.

How do you make your life too small for yourself?

It is from numberless diverse acts of courage and belief that human history is shaped. Each time a man stands up for an ideal, or acts to improve the lot of others, or strikes out against injustice, he sends forth a tiny ripple of hope, and crossing each other from a million different centers of energy and daring, those ripples build a current that can sweep down the mightiest walls of oppression and resistance.

—Robert F. Kennedy

May you memorize your moments of sweetness
and plant them on the island of your heart.

Unimagined Bridges

How do we walk through the door of rage to find the passion we fear and yearn for most? Rage is passion without choice. You become its involuntary passenger. But what is the point at which you still have choice? Does rage just happen to you? Can something on the outside make you feel that way, make you do what you do not choose to do? Can you "control" yourself and the world enough to never feel anger or rage?

I think of all the people since the beginning of time who have felt the energy we call rage. Because none of us know how to befriend this energy, it spins off into words or actions that cause abuse and suffering. But when I remember that all rage is like my rage, I can find the comfort of a shared humanity.

What if, in times of conflict or anger, we released every story we tell ourselves about who is right and who is wrong, who is bad and who is good? What if you were to stand still as your fire rises and do nothing but notice the sensations in your body? What if you were to stand there long enough to notice your breath rise and fall, long enough to notice the space before and after every inhalation and do nothing more than ask yourself, "What is really needed now?" "What am I trying to protect, to change, to create?"

How could the twisted seeds of rage you inherited be transformed so they would burn in a wholesome way for you and the rest of us?

In times of crisis, people reach for meaning. Meaning is strength. Our survival may depend on our seeking and finding it.

—Victor Frankl

May you find the courage you need to imagine rage
becoming an outrageous possibility of sanity
that lies deeper than habit or thought.

Sheltering Fear

Fear is passion without breath. To be fully alive, we have no choice but finally to move closer toward what we habitually veer away from. What if you could bring what you are most afraid of right into the hearth of your awareness, instead of ignoring it and allowing it to become an undifferentiated mass of demons that gang up on you in the dark? When you do this, fear can no longer rule you from the shadows.

There is something highly passionate about living in conscious relationship to fear. You can practice daily by venturing into the unknown and risking a reach. Not just any old reach. Only interesting ones. You can do it with paint on blank paper, not trying to make anything, but rather just for the experience of noticing what happens on that edge of uncertainty, what emerges from the black hole of the unknown. You can just sit still with your eyes, hands and ears empty, letting your thoughts warp, floating in the space between your breaths, your periphery getting wider and wider as it does at the seashore.

These little practices with risk and reach, at the edge of the unknown, give you daily shots of vitality, a pump of adrenaline. Everything else disappears, including any notion of who you are supposed to be. There is only the experience of being passionately alive. Still, each time, prior to setting out, fear may seem more justified than trust. The challenge is to keep your horizon open, to keep exploring that green, growing edge.

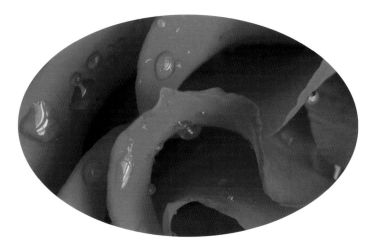

What would it be like to befriend fear with wonder,
as if it were a deer in the woods?

And then, who knows? Perhaps we will be taken in hand by
certain memories as if by angels.
—M. Yourcenar

May you embrace fear as if it were an infant in need of refuge.

Landscape of Your Heart

When I die, I want my heart and soul fully seeded with rich stories and experiences. I want to be moving forward, falling upward, leaving my body well worn. I want to be able to stay present with what is hard until it softens, with what is narrow until it expands. I want to know how to float in the silences between breaths and thoughts. I want to know how to lift above and sink below the flow of life, to drift and dream in the currents of what cannot be known. It's not that I want to be prepared for death. I want to be full of life and spilling over. I want to be so well practiced in crossing thresholds that dying is merely another opportunity to step over. I want to be so comfortable with stillness and silence that I can surrender completely to them.

What are the conditions that would
enable you to feel the heat of your heart as a prayer?
How do you have to live so you will die with your heart free?

If we are really honest with ourselves, we must admit that our lives are all that really belong to us, so it is how we use our lives that determines what kind of persons we are. And it is my deepest belief that only by giving our lives do we find life. I am convinced that the truest act of courage, the strongest act of humanity is to sacrifice ourselves for something higher—that which we believe in and love deeply.

—Cesar Chavez

May what you most love be stronger
and more powerful than anything you fear.

Let Your Wounds Be Your Teachers

How do we reignite our passion after immense loss and grief? This isn't something we achieve or even earn. Crisis can force us deep enough to find the source of whatever we truly love. The deeper the channel that pain carves into our souls, the greater the capacity we have to allow the river of joy to run through us.

Loss strips away so much. Yet it can leave us with the understanding that the art of living passionately means learning to engage both the risk to reach as well as the grace of surrender. The life force that throbs so vibrantly in each of our cores can pull us forward through every dark tunnel. Grief demands that we let go of what is no more and hold on to what can be ours forever.

Loss can help us loosen our grip on all understandings of ourselves and the world so they can be rearranged into a higher and wider order. Loss can help us find and know our own strength as well as life's fragility.

Loss can help us find what we truly value. It is in this realization we find the source of our passion inside, and therefore it is within our sphere of influence to rekindle. Most of all, loss of any kind brings with it the understanding of how much we really need each other.

What are the losses of objects, people, or dreams
that enabled you to know who you are and what you stand for?

Life is a flow. Without its banks there could be no river. Without loss, constraints, suffering pressing against your dreams, giving shape and direction to your destiny, you could never reach the sea.

—Rollo May

May the grief of loss teach you how to live so that you love your life.

The Art of the Possible

Milton Erickson, M.D., beloved clinical hypnotherapist, used to tell his students that the best way to work with people having a problem is to find their historical pattern of success and help them connect to it when they're having difficulty. When we're stuck, you can bet we have been pointing out to ourselves what's wrong and thinking of ways to fix it instead of building on what is working. The simplest indicator of the ineffectiveness of this is noticing your energy level. Focus on what hasn't worked for you today and your energy will flatten or sink. Focus on the best of what you did today, and your vitality level will go up. I don't know about you, but if I were empress of the world and wanted people to find and live according to their purpose, I'd give them good feelings, and when they were off course, I'd give them a sense of emptiness and numbness.

When in the past have you felt at your best while
achieving something you were proud of?

What does this reveal about what's really important to you?

---

*My students say "We're tired of loving." And I say, if you're
tired of loving, then you haven't really been loving,
because when you are loving, you have more strength.*

—bell hooks

May your past successes seed your future possibilities in profusion.

What Have You Been Given with Which to Give?

Most of us are reasonably articulate about our deficits and weaknesses—how many we got wrong on our spelling tests, how many things we have failed to accomplish during any given day. We become fluent at explaining our incompetencies but look straight at our gifts and talents, muttering "Oh that old thing?" This leaves us awkward and confused about how to bring our assets and resources to the rest of the community. Too many of us believe we don't matter, that what we do doesn't really make a difference.

When any of us are stuck only noticing our limitations, we are disconnected from our sense of purpose. No small wonder—from the time we begin school, if not sooner, we are taught to be blind to our assets and only see our deficits. We are carefully marked on how many we got wrong on a test and rarely, if ever, asked how we knew how to spell the ones we got right. By the time we are adults, we are well versed in every one of our limitations, skilled in our incompetence.

What are your inner gifts and talents

What have you been given with which to give?

Where do your talents and the needs of the world intersect?

What would have to happen for them to dance with each other?

Argue for your limitations and they are yours.
—Milton Erickson, M.D.

May you use your gifts and talents on behalf of
what matters most to you in a way that sustains life.

Way Opens, Way Closes

Our limitations as well as our gifts can be great indicators of where and how we should be living our purpose. None of us can do everything—the skill is in knowing how to capitalize on our strengths and allowing our limitations to indicate what *not* to give. We cannot all do everything. It is not in the nature of every seed to be an oak tree, an eggplant, a rosebush. It is not in my nature to bloom within a greenhouse. I am a wildflower, a weed perhaps. I need open and untamed spaces to sprout. I need to ask the questions and think the thoughts that others overlook.

The blessing of understanding our limitations as well as our gifts is that we realize we need each other. We need people who can flourish within institutions as well as outside of then. We need people who can think in formulas and we need people who can think in stories. We need people who can play a cello in the midst of heartache and we need people who can paint the posters that remind the rest of us it is possible. Ultimately, we have no choice. We need each other.

What people, events, situations deplete your energy right now?

What are the influences and activities that cause you to shine?

....

We are all meant to shine, as children do. As we let our own light shine, we unconsciously give other people permission to do the same. As we are liberated from our own fear, our presence automatically liberates others.

—Nelson Mandela

....

May all who are different bring their unique gifts
to the community and know they belong.

Where Are You Meant to Be Shining?

Aristotle said that one's purpose is merely a matter of knowing where one's talents and the needs of the world intersect. The ancients recognized that cultivating, developing, and setting free one's gifts was the essential labor of one's life.

In the thousands of moments that string together to make up our lives, there are some when time seems to change its shape and a certain light falls across our ordinary path. Looking back, we might describe these moments as times when we were at our best, when the gifts we were born with and the talents we have developed were braided with what we love and the needs of the world.

What does fulfillment feel like in your body?

How can you access and strengthen your gifts with
the same fervor you fix and correct your limitations?

---

*Purpose is the place where your deep gladness meets
the world's needs.*

—Frederick Buechner

May you become an ambassador for whatever
you love and create communities of commitment.

Cultivating Trust

What if the moments of the greatest wounding in your life were also places where the Divine crossed your path and the unquenchable dream you long for was born? There is nothing that drives the human mind more than what is called an "incomplete gestalt"—an unmet need for closure of some kind. Imagine seeing a pad of paper lying near you with nothing drawn on the page but a circle that is not closed. Imagine hearing just this much of the song, "Jingle bells, jingle bells, jingle all. . . ." Imagine an itch in a very sensitive place that you cannot reach. Purpose, ultimately, is the drive to close that circle, finish that song, scratch that itch, bridge that gap.

Our pain is often the aperture through which we thrust ourselves to make contributions so that others will not have to suffer the way we did. In this way, we complete the gestalt and shape the world into a place we can trust again.

What wound in your life has been a passageway to your purpose?

How could its healing provide a connection
to the healing of the world?

From the seed grows a root, then a sprout; from the sprout,
the seedling leaves; from the leaves, the stem; around the
stem, the branches; at the top, the flower. . . . We cannot say
that the seed causes the growth, nor that the soil does. We
can say that the potentialities for growth lies within the
seed, in mysterious life forces, which, when properly fos-
tered, take on certain forms.

—*M. C. Richards,*
Centering in Pottery, Poetry and the Person

May your soul crawl from hiding places of shame and
gaze upon the mystery of healing that cannot be explained.

Composting

If your purpose is only about you, it has no branches. If it is only about the rest of the world, it has no roots. This is why learning through the wounds in our history, the moments when our essential needs were not met in some very basic ways, are moments that stand still in our memory and moments that hold possibility for you to unfurl your gifts. Wouldn't it be a good joke if the worst that has happened to you holds the possibility of bringing the best in you to the community?

We become accustomed to identifying ourselves as nouns—as small, enclosed, exclusive, and local units—artist, friend, mother, victim. We spend so much time close to the canvas, carefully painting tiny purple dots in a Pointillist painting, that we have forgotten how to step back enough to get a sense of the whole. Yet it is only from this distance that we can see the overall patterns we have been creating, the verbs we have been living—creating, mothering, befriending—that are the horizons we need to move toward.

How could the worst that has happened to you
hold the possibility of bringing out the best in you?

---

*When one is a stranger to oneself, then one is estranged
from others. . . . Only when one is connected to one's core
is one truly connected to others.*

—Anne Morrow Lindbergh

May all of your wounds and broken dreams be salved.

The Gasp Where God Can Enter

Someone once told me every haiku poem has to have a gasp where God can enter. Every *life,* I think, has to have a gasp where God can enter. And every such gasp is a finger pointing to what you've spent your whole life loving. You grow stronger in the act of loving something. It sustains you. It generates energy. It is the soil of your faith. If you are depleted or feel as if you've failed, ultimately it is because you have not been living in service to what you love. In some way, therefore, you've lost your faith. Remembering vividly what you love and professing your faith in it reconnects you to the divinity of life itself.

I have faith that every child, every human has a gift, specific seeds in their soul they are meant to bring to the larger community, and they deserve to have unlimited access to that gift. I have faith that each of us brings a unique value to the larger whole. This is my profession. If I give it voice and energy to this, every one of the days of my life will count for something. If not, every day will be wasted.

In what do you profess faith?

Love is a high inducement to ripen, to become world, to become world for oneself and for another's sake, it is a great exacting claim upon you, something that chooses you out and calls you to vast things.

—Rainer Maria Rilke

May you live your dreams with dignity so you may pass them on to those who turn to you for their future.

The Still-Hungry Heart

Ultimately, we get to keep on practicing opening our hearts to the raw stuff of life, the stuff that every human being experiences, the energy we label as fear and rage, pain and ecstasy. You can't get rid of any of it. You can only come to know it with tenderness and honesty. Most of us who are human suffer from a lack of compassion and mercy for ourselves and each other. We need to learn to observe with passion, to think with patience, and to live with care.

We begin and end in authenticity, and in between, our task is to find ways to make that authenticity relevant to the world. There is nothing more precious that any of us can give than love. We forget all of that more often than we remember, and then we get to practice some more. And, hopefully, we will keep practicing, pressing vitality out of every last moment, until we die with a still-hungry heart.

Who and what do you love so much that in
expressing it you find a kind of grace in the world?

---

*Wonder is unknowing experienced as pleasure. Wonder is
not curiosity. Wonder is to curiosity what ecstasy is to mere
pleasure. Wonder is not astonishment either. Astonishment is
too brief. The only limit to the duration of wonder is the
limit of our ability to stay open.*

—David James Duncan

May we respond to the call of our passion
and find the courage to follow its path.

You Do Not Stand Alone

Living on purpose requires us to find what we love fiercely, give it all we've got, and then pass it on, as if it were a torch, to those who follow. My friend, Nancy Margulies, told me once about her grandfather, who explained to her that when a person dies, he or she has the opportunity to bequeath a legacy of love. He loved her so completely that he passed it on to her uncle, who expressed his own love for her plus that willed to him by her grandfather. Thus death never interrupts the shelter of love.

You stand on your own two feet, but you do not stand alone. So many stand behind you. So many beings have sacrificed that you may stand here. So many will come after you whose lives may be fuller, richer, wider, and deeper because you risk living what you love. What you love ennobles you. What no one loves vanishes. What even one of us loves fiercely will survive.

What's unfinished for you to learn?

What's unfinished for you to experience?

What's unfinished for you to heal?

What's unfinished for you to give?

Even here, in the silence of this room, I am not alone. This silence is alive with the unfolding of other lives and with the turning and movement of the Earth. I began to sense my connection to the world's pain and my part in healing it. I realized that my transformation of pain into love was an act of service for humankind. By embracing my existence, I could bring courage to others to face their own pain and to acknowledge what it had to teach them.

—Yael Betheim, The Unhealed Life

May you remember those who passed on to you
the seeds of their dreams so you might grow.

Your Lineage and Legacy of Love

Innovation is the trademark of our species. In order to become a doer and a maker, it is necessary that the mind's attention become enthralled by something. In order to become a maker of books, one must first fall in love with a book. Then another. We all learn through curiosity and attention, by confrontation and imitation. As children, our first experience of falling in love with a book or a stone or a river makes its way across the landscape of our still-forming mind and can be the most important, emotive, influential experience to shape our destiny and purpose.

What lights us up never truly abandons us. We abandon it. If purpose is like a river, an energy similar to water, then think of your capacity as a hose and your mind as a nozzle to direct that flow of energy. If you feel empty and focus on filling yourself up to get satisfaction, it is like trying to get energy from others to fill the hose. We forget that the source of the energy, purpose, is from a spring larger than we can ever imagine, and that it is by spilling over that we are the most fulfilled. When you are

empty and think you need to feel loved, for instance, what you may really need is to express love out into the world in some way that is meaning- ful to you.

What do you believe you have come here to give to the rest of us? What is really important for you to give voice to?

While you have a thing it can be taken from you . . . but when you give it, no robber can take it from you. It will be yours always.

—James Joyce

May you find the courage to offer yourself fully to what has heart and meaning for you.

Risking Your Significance

Your values are an activating intelligence in your life, guiding you toward the noble tasks that are yours alone to fulfill. There are moments in all of our lives that reveal these values. Their significance lies not only in what meaning we make of them, but also in what we allow those moments to make of us.

The Native peoples tell a story about Spider Woman, who emerges in times of powerful transition, pulling apart the threads that formed the old world and spinning stories that will bring new forms into existence. Think of her as the part of each of us who cares deeply about what really matters, the part that insists we live our values rather than just talk about them. Lived values are like webs, strung between the great and ordinary people of our daily existence. Consider how many women have been midwives of the possible for you, how many men have been the drops of dew clinging to those strands, how many hidden hands have reached out to you across dark abysses.

Who believes in you no matter what?

What is it about being alive you most love?

For what would you be willing to take a stand?

How are you willing to risk your significance?

Our lives begin to end the day we become silent about things that matter.

—Martin Luther King Jr.

May you value that which is plentiful.

Landscapes of Your Soul

In Hebrew there is a wonderful phrase, *tikkun olam.* It means "repairer of the world's soul." As I understand the story from which the phrase comes, it says that every day, the world's soul becomes unraveled in some way and each of us is the mender of it. It is as if we all hold, with both hands, the edge of a blanket that covers the world. It is the responsibility of each of us to repair our edge of the blanket as far as we can reach.

Each of us is a miracle of uniqueness. Each of us, therefore, is responsible for cultivating the full fertility of our soul and all it has to give to the world.

What is the legacy that you would like to leave
that would enable others to live bigger lives than you have?

*I knew growing up that I was supposed to be the things
I learned in the stories: compassionate, honorable, and
brave. . . . I knew this because the storytellers lived the
lessons they imparted in the stories.*

—Joseph M. Marshall III

May you realize you are a promise Life made to itself.

Held by Hidden Hands

We recognize purpose in solitude, but we can only feel fulfilled when we are sharing our gifts in a community. Purpose insists that we be connected to both the interior and the exterior worlds. But, but, but . . . how can this be possible? How can we support both our inner and outer lives? For so many of us, living with an external orientation has become a deeply ingrained habit. Our culture insists we compartmentalize our inner life, walling it off from the practical skills necessary to manage "out there."

All of that is true and still, no matter what, your inner life is calling you. Turning toward it, you can find yourself in a place that is beyond ego, beyond even the notion of "I." You can find yourself connected to what author Parker Palmer calls "the community we share beneath the broken surface of our lives," those others who, in this very moment, are also searching and risking to reach beyond the limitations of their previous history and create possibilities that will liberate all of us.

Who and what are you serving?

How can you achieve balance in your life?

Celie, tell the truth, have you ever found God in church? I never did. I just found a bunch of folks hoping for him to show up. Any God I ever felt in church I brought in with me. And I think all the other folks did too. They come to church to share God, not find him.

—Alice Walker

May you create stories that will help you
actively engage with your present and our future.

Regeneration

Since the invention of the Hubble telescope, if not before, we know that we belong to much larger worlds than we can even imagine. We know that we are not replaceable parts of a machine. We know we are unique living systems, interconnected and interdependent with other living systems. We know that everything within us is capable of decay—matter, beliefs, passion—and we know that anything capable of decay is also capable of regeneration.

What if we thought of ourselves like the moon, and had equal faith in what was ready to fade away as we do in what is shining? What if we could shed the known and comfortably habitual ways in which we think of ourselves and the world in order to foster the things within that are still dormant? What if you gave yourself three days a month or three hours a day to allow everything you know about yourself to disappear instead of assuming you were falling apart or clinically depressed? What if you broke through your mundane level of thinking and nested yourself in a rich, dark, regenerative soil where you could be engaged in an innocent inquiry with who you are and what you are becoming?

How would you live if you knew the date you were going to die?

What are the natural rhythms that nurture your body and soul?

I handle the notes as well as anyone; it's the pauses that count.

—Arthur Rubenstein

May you find the soil in which the seeds of your dreams can germinate into a life that is free of the limitations of your previous history.

Who and What Are You Serving?

Think of yourself as a gardener. You have been given some seeds. You don't actually grow them. You merely provide the conditions in which they can thrive and then tend them with curiosity and kindness as they grow themselves. You don't explain to the apple tree that it shouldn't be shedding leaves now, or that it should be producing pears instead, or that its flowers are excessive for the amount of fruit necessary for regeneration. A gardener cultivates a tree by acting on its essential behalf, by making sure it has the spaciousness and support necessary to find opportunities for growth in both darkness and light.

What if we realized that instead of "things" getting better and better if we work harder and harder, we realized that like a seed, we will, each in our own rhythm, go through an endless cycle of gestation, birth, growth, death, and renewal? There is no part of creation that does not go through

this cycle of falling away, disappearing, and reemerging. Think of a tree or the moon. Why should humans be the one aspect of life that is exempt?

Consider your own passion for a moment. Is it hiding under the softest fall of snow, or is it going through a raw shedding? Is your sense of purpose trembling with spring green, or flaming in full harvest?

How can you stay aligned with the natural rhythms
that nurture your body and soul?

What are the environments that bring out the best of who you are?

---

*The human brain is hardwired to connect; it is capable
of growing new synaptic connections and new neurons
through experiences and relationships. It is here we can
have our greatest impact.*

—Daniel Siegel, M.D.

May amazement and grace be your daily companions.

Letting Go of the Forgetting of Joy

In West Africa, there is a saying that it's the heart that lets go and the hands that follow. I'm coming to understand that there is no such thing as finding one's purpose. Rather, what is needed is to create the conditions for six months or six minutes where your purpose can find you. It's not about asking about the meaning of life, but rather asking what your life means. It's being willing to receive the truth of what you hear. It's asking your heart what your life is asking of you, and allowing your hands to follow.

How could you love this day as if you had never been hurt?

Some things matter because we choose to make them matter. What might make a difference to us, I think, is whether in our tiny roles, in our brief time, we inhabit life gently and add more beauty than ugliness.

—James G. March

May you release your heart and allow your hands to follow.

If Not Now, Then When?

Let us swing wide all the doors and windows of our hearts
on their rusty hinges
so we may learn how to open to life.
Let us see the light in the other and honor it
so we may lift one another on our shoulders
and carry each other along.
Let holiness move in us
so we may pay attention to its small voice
and give ourselves to life fully with both hands.

About the Author

Dawna Markova, Ph.D., is internationally known for her groundbreaking research in the fields of learning and perception. She is CEO of Professional Thinking Partners and a research member of the Society for Organizational Learning. She holds a Ph.D. in education and psychology from Union Graduate School. In 2003, Dawna co-founded SmartWired.org, a website devoted to helping kids and young adults worldwide bring out their best in all areas of life.

As one of the editors of the Random Acts of Kindness series, she helped launch a national movement to help counter America's crisis of violence. She is the author of *Spot of Grace, I Will Not Die An Unlived Life, The Smart Parenting Revolution, The Open Mind* book and audio series, *No Enemies Within, How Your Child IS Smart, Unused Intelligence,* and *Learning Unlimited.* At conferences around the world, Dawna has given inspiring keynote speeches on a wide range of topics, including finding purpose and passion, asset-focused parenting, organizational learning, living with cancer, and empowering individuals, groups and nations.

Dawna was recently honored with the Visions to Action Award, "for people who have made a profound contribution to the world." A long-term cancer survivor (she was told she had six months to live almost thirty years ago), Dawna has appeared on numerous TV programs and is a frequent guest on National Public Radio and New Dimensions radio. You can contact her at: *www.Dawnamarkova.com* and *www.Ptpinc.org.*